DATE DUE

DEC 26 91			
JAN 23 92			
11-1			
NOV 29 '93			
JAN 21 '94			
MAY 23 '94			
10-20-94			
12/16/94			
JUN 13 '97			
OCT 11 '99			
GAYLORD			PRINTED IN U.S.A.

STIFF EARS
*Animal Folktales of the
North American Indian*

STIFF EARS

Animal Folktales of the
North American Indian

WRITTEN AND ILLUSTRATED BY

ALEX WHITNEY

HENRY Z. WALCK, INC.   NEW YORK

Library of Congress Cataloging in Publication Data
Whitney, Alex.
　Stiff ears.
　SUMMARY: A collection of animal legends from the
Hopi, Pawnee, Chinook, Chippewa, Iroquois, and Cherokee
Indians.
　1. Indians of North America—Legends. 2. Animals,
Legends and stories of—Juvenile literature.
[1. Indians of North America—Legends. 2. Animals—
Fiction] I. Title.
E98.F6W5　　398.2'452'09701　　74-6029
ISBN 0-8098-2103-6

In memory of He-on-won-tha

Contents

Southwest
THE HOPI

The Hopi, or *Hopitu,* "The Peaceful Ones," built their villages on seven mesas in what is now northeastern Arizona. Each village was divided into clans, and each clan was governed by a chieftain who was also the spiritual leader. The tribe lived in mud-covered stone houses of three and four stories high, entered by ladders.

In addition to their crops of maize, one of the Hopi's main sources of food was small game, particularly the jackrabbit which they hunted with a type of boomerang called a "rabbit stick."

Many present-day Hopi still practice the arts and crafts and the religion of their ancestors. Now, as then, they hold their ceremonial rain dances and secret rites in an underground chamber called a *kiva.*

Hopi mythology is closely tied to the rules of behavior set by the tribe nearly two thousand years ago. The legend of *Stiff Ears,* for example, illustrates an ancient Hopi principle: Always be ready to listen to those older in experience.

Stiff Ears

A HOPI LEGEND

Far beyond the Sacred Mesas is a desert plain of wind-carved stones and sand, strewn with shrubs and cactus plants. This is the dwelling place of a tribe of many jack-rabbits. Some of the Old Ones of the tribe still remember Stiff Ears, a rabbit who once lived in one of their villages. Stiff Ears, they recall, was more impatient and more head-strong than the others in his clan.

One morning Stiff Ears and his brother Wise One set off on their daily hunt for prickly cactus pears and sagebrush leaves. As the sun climbed higher and scorched the land below, the brothers decided to rest in the shade of a dense clump of spiny cactus

11

plants. Wise One, drowsy from the shimmering desert heat, soon fell asleep. It was then that Stiff Ears made a surprising discovery. He found he could see through the cactus thicket into a magical world beyond—a world filled with juicy prickly pears growing in a meadow of thick green grass.

"Wake up, Wise One!" cried Stiff Ears, his eyes shining with excitement. "I've just seen a beautiful world beyond the cactus thicket! It's full of good food, much thicker, juicier and greener than we have here. That's where we'll live with our clan, and those who don't belong to us we'll leave behind."

Stiff Ears bounded off to tell his clan the news of his discovery. But Wise One remained by the deep-rooted cactus thicket. The longer he gazed at the sharply pointed thorns on its fleshy leaves, the more he wondered if it would be well to go into the country Stiff Ears had seen. Wise One decided to ask the advice of his village chief-

tain, an older rabbit whose name was Experience.

When Wise One found Experience and told him about the morning's events, Experience said: "Stiff Ears has seen only what is through the cactus thicket, but he hasn't thought about how to reach the world he has seen. Since it would be foolish to go through a cactus thicket, there is only one safe path to that country — the rocky trail around the thicket. Tell Stiff Ears a short-cut of any sort could be dangerous."

Wise One scampered off to the sandy hollow where his clan lived, and repeated what Experience had said. But Stiff Ears laughed scornfully. "Everyone knows it would be foolish to go *through* a thorny cactus thicket!" he exclaimed impatiently. "But why should we waste time in going *around* it? I've thought of a much quicker and cleverer way to reach our new homeland. We'll travel *under* the thicket!"

Although Wise One and the other rabbits in the clan reminded Stiff Ears of Experience's warning against taking a shortcut, Stiff Ears stubbornly refused to listen. "If I must, I'll go on the journey alone!" he shouted. "I know it's a safe journey!"

Whereupon Stiff Ears dug a tunnel from his sandy hollow. At first the way was easy and his progress was swift. But just as he was underneath the thorny cactus thicket, thinking about all the good grass and prickly pears soon to be his, he suddenly found he could go no further. Neither could he return. He was in darkness, surrounded by the rocks and large stones which had caved in his tunnel. He realized too late they had fallen because of his burrowing in the loose, sandy soil.

So there to this day is Stiff Ears, trapped in a pit of his own digging. And there he will remain for many moons beyond tomorrow.

Midwest Woodlands
THE CHIPPEWA

The Chippewa lived in bark-covered wigwams in the territory extending from North Dakota eastward to the shores of Lake Huron. The tribe were master canoe-builders and canoeists. Game hunting, berrying and wild-rice gathering were their principal means of obtaining food during the warmer months; in winter they speared fish through holes cut in the ice.

The Chippewa were known for their picture writing. One of the many animal symbols they engraved on their scrolls of birch bark and deerskin was the tortoise, which they described as "a creature wise and patient. He stretches out his neck and looks first to the right, then to the left, then straight ahead. If no danger is in sight, he proceeds forward. His top and bottom shells are as two moons joined together. Within these moons is great wisdom. When there is danger, the tortoise shelters in his moons."

Chippewa folktales were used to instruct, as well as to entertain. The legend of *A Jump Ahead,* for instance, reminded the tribe that one's best weapon was wisdom, or the use of one's head.

17

A Jump Ahead

A CHIPPEWA LEGEND

Among the darkly wooded hills, the Lake of *Mishoshu,* the magician, glittered palely. Ranks of tall reeds rimmed its pebbly shores, and fleets of water lilies grew in its shallow inlets. Perched on one of the broad lily pads was a bullfrog who stared curiously at a tortoise on the shore.

"Doesn't your thick shell prevent you from jumping to safety when danger threatens?" the frog asked the tortoise.

"There's no reason for me to jump," replied the tortoise. "Whenever I need protection, I simply withdraw into my shell."

"But jumping out of reach of one's enemy is the only sure means of escape," insisted

19

the frog. "You should learn to jump the way I do."

Now while the frog and the tortoise were talking, a long-legged blue heron stole through the reeds to the water's edge. She was extremely hungry, and when she heard the deep voice of the frog, she waded swiftly into the water. Thrusting her long beak beneath the lily pads, she seized the frog by his hind legs. The frog gave a frightened croak and struggled in vain to free himself. But just as the heron was about to swallow her victim, she heard the sharp bark of a fox close by. The startled bird dropped the frog, who splashed into the water and swam away unharmed.

The heron tilted her head to one side and looked uneasily at the shore, but the only creature she saw was the tortoise. Puzzled, she waded ashore and pecked rudely on the tortoise's shell. "Tell me," she demanded, "did you hear a fox bark a moment ago?"

"I must have heard it," said the tortoise, "since it was I who barked to keep you from swallowing my friend."

"You'll pay for making me go hungry!" screeched the heron, furious she had been tricked so easily. "I'll snatch you in my beak, fly to the tallest treetop and leave you on the highest branch!"

"Splendid!" said the tortoise. "I'd like nothing better than a bird's-eye view of the lake!"

"In that case, I'll snatch you in my beak, fly over the shore and drop you on the pebbles!" declared the heron, pleased with her cleverness.

"Splendid!" said the tortoise. "Bouncing on pebbles toughens my shell!"

"In that case," shrieked the heron, "I'll carry you out in the lake and drown you!"

The tortoise drew his head into his shell. "Oh no!" he wailed in a muffled voice. "That is the worst thing you could do to me!"

The heron hastily snatched the tortoise in her beak, waded into the lake and dropped him into the water, where he sank like a stone. Squawking triumphantly, the heron flapped her wings and flew awkwardly away.

After a time, the frog settled himself once again on his favorite lily pad and gazed at the glassy surface of the lake. Presently the water was gently stirred, and the head of the tortoise peered cautiously above it.

"You're still alive!" exclaimed the frog, his eyes bulging with astonishment. "Fortunately for you, the fox ate the heron! However," he added, "you may not always be lucky. You should learn to jump to safety, the way I do!"

"The only thing you've jumped to, so far, is the wrong conclusion!" snapped the tortoise. And he dove and swam underwater toward a floating log.

Northeast
THE IROQUOIS

Four centuries ago, the Cayuga, Mohawk, Onandaga, Oneida and Seneca clans of the Iroquois tribe banded together to form a union known as the Five Great Nations. This powerful group controlled the region between the Hudson and Ohio Rivers and the land east and south of Lakes Erie and Ontario. There they lived in rectangular, bark-covered "long-houses" in villages often protected by moats and fences made of tall, wooden poles.

The family life of each clan centered about a woman, who served as their decision-maker. Women collected roots and berries and tended their crops of maize, squash, beans and melons. The men hunted, fished and produced syrup and sugar from the maple trees.

Most Iroquois folktales, seldom without a moral, were based on the tribe's observance of nature. They likened the behavior of animals, fish and birds to the strengths and weaknesses of human beings. Typical of Iroquois animal legends is *The Porcupine Snowball,* a story which advised listeners that it is not always wise to imitate another.

The Porcupine Snowball

AN IROQUOIS LEGEND

From his lofty perch in the spruce tree, *Onheto*, the porcupine, gazed at the blanket of snow the Spirit of Winter had spread across the land. On the glistening, white hillside opposite his tree, Onheto saw the paw prints of his enemy *Mishogum*, the gray wolf. Mishogum's tracks led down to his den in a hollow near the bottom of the hill.

Presently Onheto caught sight of a river otter, loping over the hillcrest. Suddenly the otter hurled himself on his stomach. Then, with his legs and webbed feet spread backwards, he slid rapidly downhill like a toboggan. When he reached the bottom, he

plunged into a snowdrift and emerged several otter-lengths away in a puff of snow, snorting with glee.

"If an otter can slide downhill with such ease, then surely a porcupine can, too!" Onheto told himself.

Onheto climbed down the spruce tree and waddled to the foot of the hill. As he lurched up the slope, his stocky body and thick tail plowed furrows in the deep, soft snow. By the time he had struggled to the top, tufts of snow clung to his woolly under-fur and to the long hairs and quills on his back and his tail. Just then a strong gust of wind pushed him forward, and he began to roll slowly downhill. As he went faster and faster, he began to resemble a giant snowball. Soon he was hurtling down the hillside on a direct course toward the entrance of Misho-gum's den.

Mishogum, dozing in his snug winter lair, dreamed he had cornered Onheto at the base of the fir tree. The wolf licked his chops in his sleep, looking forward to the porcupine dinner in store for him. His pleasure was short-lived. A frosty, white ball rolled into him and jolted him awake. Mishogum sprang up on all fours and let out a blood-curdling howl. "How did a ball of snow filled with nasty little twigs and brambles find its way in here?" he yelped. "I must get rid of it, before it melts in my warm, dry den!" With his head and his forepaws, Mishogum pushed and rolled the snow-laden porcupine out of his home. "All this activity has made me hungrier than ever!" snarled the wolf. But since he was sure Onheto must be out of reach on a branch of the spruce tree, Mishogum decided to go back to sleep.

Outside Mishogum's den, Onheto shook himself vigorously, shedding most of the snow and a few loose quills. He looked behind him fearfully to make sure the gray wolf was nowhere in sight. Then he shuffled as fast as he could to the spruce tree, and briskly pulled himself up the trunk with his long, sharp claws.

"The Great Spirit gave me weapons with which to climb and quills with which to protect myself," Onheto thought. "Hereafter, I'll do only the things which the porcupine knows how to do, for the Great Spirit never meant me to slide!"

Onheto gnawed contentedly on the bark of the spruce and listened to its topmost branches creak and sigh in the wind.

Northwest

THE CHINOOK

The Chinook lived in gable-roofed houses of cedar planks in the Columbia River area of northern Oregon and southern Washington. For most of the year, they occupied small villages along the rugged Pacific coast and among the inland marshes and evergreen forests. But each spring, when the salmon were migrating to their spawning grounds, the tribesmen moved to temporary campsites near a series of waterfalls on the Columbia River. There they built huge fish-drying sheds for the salmon, which they caught with spears and long-handled nets.

The Chinook were noted merchants. They paddled their dugout canoes, brimming with fur pelts and dried fish, to trading posts as far away as Vancouver.

The salmon and the trout have often been featured in Chinook folklore. When a *Tye-yea*, the village Headman and Storyteller, related the legend of *The Journey*, he began by speaking about the rainbow trout. "They are stout-hearted fish," the Tye-yea reminded his listeners, "and they have never forgotten the lesson their forefather learned from the salmon: Always go forward; never despair."

The Journey

A CHINOOK LEGEND

On a day near the beginning of things, Tenas the small rainbow trout decided to explore the waters beyond his calm, clear pond. He had heard many tales of the river from the bull trout who had once been there.

"A strange and wonderful place is the river," the bull trout had told Tenas. "But beware of fierce fish hawks and of toothy largemouth bass. Both tribes are always on the warpath, preying on small fish."

Despite the bull trout's warning, Tenas was determined to see the river for himself. So he flung himself into the Sing-song Brook that flowed from his pond.

For a time Tenas swam peacefully downstream in the brook, past grassy meadows and forests of towering cedars. Then the stream widened, and the water began to rush and tumble over a rocky bed. At first the little trout struggled bravely in the strong current. But the bubbling white water tossed him beneath the branches of fallen trees, around huge boulders and over thundering waterfalls.

At length the foaming waters of the brook carried Tenas into the wide, deep river. But when he looked about for a place in which to rest from his ordeal, his heart froze in terror. Lurking in a cavern below him was a fearsome largemouth bass. Tenas swam hastily upward, but when he reached the river's surface, he heard the shrill, hungry cries of fish hawks in the sky above him.

So overcome with panic and despair was Tenas that he scarcely noticed the silvery wake of ripples made by the salmon who swam up to him.

"Little brother, what brings you to these deep and dangerous waters?" the salmon asked in a kindly voice.

"I came here to learn many things," replied Tenas. "Instead I find myself trapped by enemies in both the sky and the river, and I haven't the strength to return upstream to my pond."

"Follow me," said the salmon. "I'm on my way from the sea to my breeding grounds in an icy mountain pool. Your pond is along the way."

As the salmon led the way out of the river and back into the Sing-song Brook, Tenas followed closely behind. Then up and up the stream they traveled—fighting against its swift currents, leaping up waterfalls and over churning rapids. Each time Tenas felt sure he hadn't the strength to go further, the salmon relentlessly urged him onward. At last—battered, bruised and exhausted— the two fish reached the more peaceful waters of the brook, and soon entered Tenas' pond.

"Now we shall be able to rest!" gasped Tenas.

"I never rest on the journey to my breeding grounds. I must leave you, for I still have a long way to go," said the salmon as he swam toward the other end of the pond.

Tenas admired the dazzling reflections of sunlight on the salmon's scales as the great fish leaped out of the water, arched his body in midair, and splashed into the brook that fed the pond.

A feeling of loneliness swept over the little trout. Then he was suddenly filled with a longing to accompany his friend to the end of his journey. "Wait, for I'm going with you!" Tenas called to the salmon. And he darted across the pond and flung himself into the softly gurgling waters of the Sing-song Brook.

Now all this happened a long time ago,

when our people were able to talk to the Finny Tribes. But perhaps you've noticed that the rainbow trout still overcome almost every obstacle on their journeys up and down our streams.

Plains
THE PAWNEE

The homeland of the Pawnee stretched from southern Nebraska to northern Kansas, once vast prairie lands over which millions of buffalo ranged. The tribe was divided into four main bands under a single head chief. Their permanent houses were circular dirt lodges, but when traveling on buffalo-hunting expeditions, they lived in portable tepees of buffalo hides draped over long, slender poles.

The buffalo was the most prized animal hunted by the Pawnees. Its meat, hide, horns, sinew and bones gave them food, clothing, shelter, fuel, tools and weapons. The tribe thought their god *Atius Tirawa* created the buffalo especially for them, and they enforced strict hunting rules for the preservation of the great herds.

The Pawnee believed a race of giants once inhabited their land, and that the eventual downfall of the race was due to their pride and lack of attention to the lesser creatures on earth. This belief is reflected in several Pawnee myths and hero-stories, including the legend of *Why the Buffalo Lost a War*.

41

Why the Buffalo Lost a War

A PAWNEE LEGEND

One day near the edge of winter, the field mouse stepped out of her nest of dried grass in the small prairie meadow. She sniffed the crisp, tangy air and knew that *Wa-zee-yah*, the north wind, would soon sweep the prairie with his frost-tipped wings. It was time, she decided, to gather her food for the long cold days and nights ahead.

While the mouse busily searched for wild beans in the tangled grass, a buffalo bull came into the meadow to graze. The sight of the huge, shaggy beast alarmed the little mouse, for she knew he would eat most of the grass and mow down the rest with his hooves and his prickly tongue. "There'll be no place left in which to hide," the mouse muttered to herself as she scurried toward her unwelcome neighbor.

"*Looah,* greetings!" said the mouse to the buffalo. "Welcome to the meadow. But remember to save a small patch of it for me, won't you?"

The buffalo, munching placidly on a mouthful of grass, ignored her.

The mouse was about to repeat her plea in a louder tone of voice when she saw the buffalo trample on her nest of dried grass.

"Ho, buffalo!" squeaked the mouse, her whiskers bristling. "Thanks to your clumsiness, you've destroyed my only protection from Wa-zee-yah! Leave this meadow at once, or I'll challenge you to a war!"

The buffalo looked with contempt at the mouse. "Don't be foolish, little one!" he snorted. "You're far too small to wage war with me, a Mighty Giant!"

A moment later, the buffalo felt a tickle

inside his right ear. He shook his head from side to side and twitched his ears back and forth, but the tickly feeling only increased. Flinging his tail in the air, he ran straight forward and then he ran in circles. When at last he stopped abruptly, the mouse jumped out of his ear and onto the ground.

The buffalo stared with surprise at the mouse. "Ho! So you're the one who's been tickling me!" he exclaimed angrily. "I'll show you what happens to little ones who show no respect for Mighty Giants!" And, lowering his massive head, the buffalo charged at his tiny tormentor. But the mouse quickly sprang on top of the buffalo's head.

Once more the buffalo felt a maddening tickle, this time inside his left ear. Bellowing with rage, he pawed the air with his front hooves and tore up the grass with his sharp horns. Then he wheeled about and galloped out of the meadow. Enveloped in clouds of dust, he plunged recklessly down a rocky hillside. When he reached the ravine below, the mouse leaped out of his ear and onto the ground.

"Do you still claim I'm too small to wage war with you, O Mighty Giant?" she called after her retreating enemy. The little mouse listened for his reply, but all she heard was the faint pounding of hooves in the distance.

Southeast
THE CHEROKEE

The Cherokee were town dwellers who farmed in the region which now includes Virginia, eastern Tennessee, northern Georgia and Alabama and the mountain areas of North and South Carolina. The tribe, which was divided into seven clans, lived in rectangular log houses roofed with the bark of the chestnut, a tree they held sacred. In each of their villages a seven-sided Council Lodge, built on an earthen mound, served as a gathering place for their religious ceremonies. Nearby were their lacrosse playing ground, their public storehouse and their community planting fields.

The village *Shaman,* or Storyteller, wove many tales around the owl, or "Watcher-in-the-Night." It was used as their symbol of wisdom, and its carved image was placed above the entrance to the Council Lodge.

The Cherokee believed they were descended from the eagle, who represented both strength and courage. The legend of *Ruler of the Air* was often told to young would-be warriors to explain why only those who had proved their bravery and might in battle were allowed to wear the eagle's feather.

49

Ruler of the Air

A CHEROKEE LEGEND

A long time ago, long before man uttered his first war-whoop, the birds quarrelled about which of them could fly the highest.

Some were sure it was the hawk. "He is a spirit of fire and ice," they claimed. "He streaks like an arrow through the air."

Others were certain it was the eagle. "He can look the sun directly in the eye," they declared. "Storms and strong winds are his playthings."

But the little dark-feathered shrike insisted he could fly higher than either the eagle or the hawk. "That would be easy for a bird as clever as I!" he boasted.

At last the great-horned owl grew tired

51

of being kept awake all day by the birds' endless bickering. "We shall settle this matter once and for all," he told them. "Tomorrow we will hold a contest. I, the oldest and wisest among you, will be the judge. Whoever flies the highest will be the winner. And the winner will be Ruler of the Air."

On the following day, all the People of the Sky—from *Hu-hu,* the mocking bird, to *Sanuwa,* the osprey—flocked together. Then the great-horned owl gave three piercing hoots, the signal for the contest to start. With loud whirrings, flurries and beating of wings, the birds took off. Each raced to climb, one above the other. The hawk flashed past them at breathtaking speed and soon mounted in the sky. But the eagle, riding on a strong current of wind, swiftly rose higher. Then his great wings sang upon the air, as he circled and dipped and soared far above the earth.

Suddenly the little shrike, who had hidden himself on the eagle's back, rose unsteadily to his feet. Firmly clutching the eagle, he flapped his wings and shrieked, "Look at me! I'm the highest! I'm the winner!"

The eagle folded his wings and sailed slowly back to earth. Then the shrike fluttered down from the eagle's back and strode over to the great-horned owl. "Here I am to claim my victory!" the shrike croaked harshly. "Tell the Feathered Tribes I'm Ruler of the Air!"

The other birds clucked and squawked and twittered excitedly until the great-horned owl spread his wings and called for silence. "The winner of our contest has flown nearer to the sun than any other bird," he announced.

The crafty shrike puffed up his feathers and proudly strutted back and forth.

"Not only has the winner *flown* the highest," continued the great-horned owl,

glaring fiercely at the shrike, "he has also carried an extra weight upon his back. There is only one of us with such great powers of flight: the mighty eagle, Ruler of the Air!"